SUZHOU

苏　州

FOREIGN LANGUAGES PRESS　BEIJING

外文出版社　北京

SUZHOU

Suzhou is one of the 24 famous historical and cultural cities in China. Its history can be traced back 6,000-7,000 years ago. Archeological finds have proven that there were already early inhabitants in the area of Suzhou during the New Stone Age. As a city, Suzhou has a history of 2,500 years. In the late Spring and Autumn Period (770-476 B.C.), the State of Wu rose in southeast China. He Lü, the King of Wu, ordered his Minister, Wu Zixu, to build a He Lü City in 514 B.C., with walls of 24 kilometers long in circumference and having eight land and water gates. This was the first city of Suzhou. It not only served as the capital of the Wu State but also as an economic and cultural center in southeast China. During its long history, Suzhou city has witnessed many changes, but the site, scale and structure of its city walls have remained almost the same. Of all the city gates, the Panmen Gate is particularly well-preserved and is the only existing typical land-and-water gate in China. On a *Map of the Pingjiang Prefecture* (during the Song Dynasty, Suzhou was named the Pingjiang Prefecture) on a Song Dynasty (960-1279) stone tablet housed in the Suzhou Stone Carvings Museum, there are six north-south rivers, 14 east-west rivers and 359 bridges depicted in the city. The names of many streets and bridges shown on the map are still in use today.

Suzhou, one of the famous tourist cities in China, has unique natural scenery. Its east side is dotted with lakes and crisscrossed by rivers, and its west is a hilly area. Mount Lingyan, Mount Tianping, and Tiger Hill rise in its western suburbs. Tiger Hill is known as the "First Scenic Spot in the State of Wu." On its plain in the eastern part are networks of rivers and lakes. The larger ones are Yangcheng Lake and Jinji Lake. About 15 kilometers to the southwest of the city is the famous Taihu Lake Scenic Area. The water from Taihu Lake flows through the city and empties into the Yangtze River. Residential houses in the city stand mostly along the rivers, and stone steps have been built from the houses down to the water. Stone bridges span the rivers one after another to connect the small streets or lanes on both banks. The distinctive features of Suzhou's scenery are its beautiful natural landscapes, graceful artistic gardens, and the poetic scenes of small rivers flowing under arched stone bridges. Marco Polo, the Italian traveler, came to China in 1275. During his stay in China, he served as an official for 17 years and covered most of the country. His *Travels*, written after his return to Italy, records that Suzhou was extremely beautiful and could rival his hometown — Venice.

Suzhou, with its mild climate, fertile farmlands and abundant products, is known as the "Land of Rice and Fish. " In Middle Ages, Suzhou already had well developed agriculture, a flourishing handicraft industry and thriving commerce. During the reign of Qing Emperor Qianlong, the court painter Xu Yang, who came from Suzhou, did a genre scroll painting titled *Prosperous Suzhou*. In the downtown section of this painting, more than 200 shops are carefully depicted to reflect the prosperous scene of Suzhou at that time. Among many of the local products of Suzhou, the most famous are the Taihu Lake whitebait, pearls, crabs from Yangcheng Lake, Biluochun green tea, and white loquats. Its well-known handicrafts include Suzhou embroidery, sandalwood fan, mahogany carving, jade carving, Taohuawu woodblock prints, and mahogany products.

Suzhou's beautiful scenery and abundant products had attracted numerous high officials, scholars, men of letters and rich merchants to come to live in Suzhou ever since ancient times. Many of them built gardens and villas in Suzhou, either for their social activities or for their retired leisure life. According to the city annals of Suzhou, there were as many as 200 private gardens in the city during the Ming and Qing dynasties (1368-1911). Hence Suzhou is known as the "Garden City. " The most famous gardens are the Surging Waves Pavilion, Lion Grove, Humble Administrator's Garden,

Lingering Garden, West Garden, Fisherman's Garden and Pleasure Garden, each representing a different architectural style of the Song, Yuan, Ming and Qing dynasties. The Suzhou gardens are not like the imperial gardens in Beijing or Chengde which were mostly built outside of the city in vast areas, using the beautiful natural landscapes to construct symmetrically arranged palace halls on a central axis. The Suzhou gardens were all private gardens, taking up very small spaces. But the architects employed miniature techniques to exquisitely put artificial hills, trees, pavilions, towers, platforms, lakes and bridges into a small area, thus creating an artistic effect of viewing big scenes in a small garden.

Today, Suzhou is heading towards modernization. Since the 1980s, Suzhou has sped up its economic and technological cooperation with foreign countries, and about 7,000 Chinese-foreign joint-venture enterprises have been set up. Suzhou has formed sister city relationships with 18 cities in Italy, Canada, Japan, the United States, France and other countries. In recent years, Suzhou has started to build its Industrial Garden with the cooperation of Singapore, and the project is going well. During this modernization process, people can still see the traditional lifestyles and folk customs in the city. Although tap water is now connected to every household, people still have the habit of walking down the stone steps behind their houses to fetch water from the river and doing their washing in the river. At sunset, small boats return to the ferry docks close to the houses, floating peacefully on the water amid the bustling life of the city. At small towns outside of the city, almost every household is engaged in sericulture, with mulberry trees planted in front of or behind their houses. Girls sit in wooden tubs floating on the ponds to gather waternuts. Fishermen row sampans on rivers and lakes, with cormorants perching on the sides of their boats.... Modern life is thus mixed with traditional and folk customs, enabling people to feel the pulse of this ancient and modern city in southeast China.

苏 州

　　苏州是中国首批公布的 24 个历史文化名城之一,它的历史可上溯到六、七千年前。从考古发掘材料看,在新石器时代苏州地区已有人类劳动、生息、繁衍。苏州建城的历史已有 2500 多年。春秋时代(公元前 770-前 476 年)后期,诸侯国吴国崛起于中国东南部。公元前 514 年,吴王阖闾命大臣伍子胥在江南平原上筑起了一座周长约 24 公里、有水陆城门各 8 座的阖闾大城,这便是苏州最早的城邑。它不仅是当时吴国的都城,而且长期以来成为江南的经济文化中心。在漫长的岁月里,苏州城虽历经沧桑变化,但基本上保持了原来的城址、规模和格局,其中盘门水陆城门保存较为完整,是中国现存最典型的一座水陆城门。从苏州碑刻博物馆现存的宋代(公元 960-1279 年)古碑《平江府图》(宋代苏州称平江府)上,还可看到宋代苏州城内,南北向的河流有 6 条,东西向的有 14 条,桥梁 359 座,图中记载的许多街道、桥梁名称,现在仍继续沿用。

　　苏州的自然景观独具特色,是著名的旅游胜地。苏州东部多水,西部多山,山明水秀,景色如画。它的西部有灵岩山、天平山、虎丘山等,山色秀丽,虎丘山号称"吴中第一名胜"。在东侧平畴上,河渠如网,串联着众多的湖泊,较大的有阳澄湖、金鸡湖等。它的西南 15 公里处就是有名的太湖风景区。太湖近苏州一侧流出的湖水纵横交叉穿过城区流入长江。市民住宅都沿河而筑,两岸建有许多水踏步和小码头,一座座石拱桥横跨河上,沟通两岸。苏州自然景观的最大特色是,既有湖光山色、烟波浩渺的气势,又有江南水乡小桥流水的诗韵。意大利旅行家马可·波罗于公元 1275 年来到中国,在元朝任官 17 年,游踪几乎遍及整个中国。他回国后在所写的《马可·波罗行记》一书中,盛赞

"苏州城漂亮得惊人"可以与他的故乡——世界著名的水上城市威尼斯媲美。

苏州地区气候适宜,土地肥沃,物产丰富,素称"江南鱼米之乡"。中世纪时,这里农业已很发达,手工业兴盛,商业繁荣。清乾隆时苏州人徐扬于公元1759年绘了一幅《姑苏繁华图卷》,画上可辨认的商店市招有二百多家,形象地反映了当时苏州的繁华景象。苏州众多的物产中,著名的有太湖银鱼、珍珠,阳澄湖大蟹,碧螺春茶叶,白沙枇杷等。苏州负有盛名的工艺品有苏绣、檀香扇、红木雕刻、玉雕、桃花坞木刻年画、红木器件等,琳琅满目,美不胜收。

如此名胜佳丽地,如此物产富饶地,从古代到近代吸引了无数达官贵人、文人墨客、富豪商贾在此居停驻足。许多人在苏州觅地营建园林别墅,或作为社会活动场所,或作怡娱暮年、悠然终老用。据苏州府志记载,明清两代(公元1368-1911年),苏州宅地园林竟多至一、二百家。因此苏州又赢得了"园林之城"的桂冠。退迩闻名的园林有沧浪亭、狮子林、拙政园、留园、西园、网师园、怡园等,分别代表宋、元、明、清四个朝代的不同风格。苏州园林不同于中国北京、承德等地的皇家园林。皇家园林多于郊外利用优美的自然山水,布局营造,面积广大;中轴线上建筑金碧辉煌的宫殿群,给人以雍容华贵之感。苏州园林是私家园林,占地面积小,匠师们多采用缩景的手法,在有限的空间内点缀假山、树木,安排亭台楼阁、池塘小桥,给人以小中见大的艺术效果。

今天,苏州正在向现代化的都市迈进。80年代以来,对外经济技术合作的步伐逐年加快,现已建成"三资"企业近7000家。苏州还与意大利、加拿大、日本、美国、法国等国18个城市缔结为友好城市。近年来,苏州与新加坡合作开发"工业园区",工程正在进行中。这些,都可以看到它昂首阔步的雄姿。在这同时,人们还是可以捕捉到一些古朴民情的镜头。尽管有了自来水,居民们还是习惯地走下屋后台阶,在河中汲水、浣洗;当夕阳西下水映霞光之际,家家小舟悠然归来,泊于房前,在城市的喧闹声中映衬着静谧和谐的气氛;在城郊、在小镇上,还可看到家家种桑、户户养蚕的景象;姑娘们坐在木盆里在池塘里采摘菱角;渔夫们驾一叶扁舟荡漾于河湖港汊间,小舟两旁排列着待命的鱼鹰……现代化的生活气息与古朴的民情民风相映成趣,人们可以从中感触到苏州历史跳动的脉息。

苏州游览图
TOURIST MAP OF SUZHOU

至上海 To Shanghai

虎丘
Tiger Hill

苏州火车站
Railway Station

外城河 Outer City River

沈兴路

平门
Pingmen Gate

拙政园
Hemble Administrator's Garden

娄门
Loumen Gate

虎丘路
Huqiu Road

广济路
Guangji Road

北塔寺
North Temple Pagoda

狮子林
Lion Grove

留园
Lingering Garden

阊门
Changmen Gate

西中市 Xizhong Shi 东中市 Dongzhong Shi 白塔西路 Baita West Road 白塔东路 Baita East Road

留园路
Liuyuan Road

人民路

中街路 Zhongjie Road

玄妙观
Xuanmiao Temple

临顿路 Jindan Road

金门路 Jinmen Road

金门
Jinmen Gate

宝德路

景德路 Jingde Road

观前街 Guanqian Street

人民路 Renmin Road

干将路

怡园
Pleasure Garden

养育巷

双塔
Twin Pagodas

干将路 Ganjiang Road

养育巷 Yangyu Lane

长江 Yangtze River

运河 Wusong River

常熟
Changshu

十梓街

十全街

石路 To Grand Canal

阳澄湖
Yangcheng Lake

苏州市
Suzhou

唯亭
Weiting

宝带桥
Jade Belt Bridge

甪直
Luzhi

吴淞江 Wusong River

漕湖 Caohu Lake

市政府
★ City Council

网师园
Fisherman's Garden

石湖街 Shizi Street

石全街 Shiquan Street

苏州饭店
Suzhou Hotel

葑门
Fengmen Gate

外城河 Outer City River

沧浪亭
Surging Wave Pavilion

木渎
Mudu

吴江
Wujiang

同里
Tongli

周庄
Zhouzhuang

上海
SHANGHAI

瑞光塔
Auspicious Light Pagoda

盘门三景
Three Sights of Panmen Gate

南门路 Nanmen Road

人民南路 Renmin South Road

南门
Nanmen Gate

西山
West Hill

东山
East Hill

太湖 Taipu River

浙江 ZHEJIANG

震泽
Zhenze

盛泽
Shengze

平望
Pingwang

Suzhou is located to the south of the Yangtze River and to the east of Taihu Lake. Outside of the city are Yangcheng, Chenghu, Jinji and Dushu lakes, and the Loujiang, Wusong and Dongjiang rivers, which connect with the Yangtze River. Suzhou has a network of waterways, so that the rural area people often use boats rather than vehicles.

苏州北临长江，西滨太湖，城外尚有阳澄湖、澄湖、金鸡湖、独墅湖，以及与太湖相通的娄江、吴淞江、东江，河湖港汊如网，在农村人们出行常以舟代车。

In the city, waterways run parallel to the streets, and residential houses are built along them. In front of the houses are streets busy with traffic, and behind them are rivers with boats of all kinds.

苏州城内水道与陆衢并行,民宅建于滨河街道的一侧,往往门前是人行车驰的街市,后窗临行舟的水巷。

12

◁ Today there are many modern buildings in Suzhou, but you can still see crisscrossed rivers, which are spanned by bridges, and the shadows of ancient pagodas in the water. The city thus keeps its ancient flavor.

今日苏州尽管不乏现代化建筑，但是市区内仍然是水巷纵横，举目见桥，古塔映空，保持着水乡古城的风貌。

The State of Wu built eight gates in its city walls 2,500 years ago. The picture shows Panmen Gate, a land-and-water gate, at the southwest corner of the city walls, which is well preserved.

2500年前，吴国建城时曾在四面城垣上辟建了八座水陆城门，图为西南面的盘门水陆城门，至今仍保持着当年的格局。

Suzhou has many ancient pagodas. Cloud Rock Temple Pagoda (*Yunyansita*) on Tiger Hill (*Huqiushan*), the symbol of Suzhou, was built in 961. It is a 47.7-meter-high brick pagoda in imitation of a wooden structure. Because of the sinking of its base, the pagoda slants a bit to one side like the Leaning Tower of Pisa in Italy. During its renovation in 1956, some precious relics were found in the pagoda such as a box of Buddhist scriptures, embroideries and bronze Buddhist images.

苏州多古塔,被视为苏州城标志的虎丘云岩寺塔,建成于公元961年,高47.7米,是一座仿木结构楼阁式砖塔。由于地基松动,塔身倾斜,如同意大利比萨斜塔。1956年整修时,在塔内发现了经箱、刺绣、铜佛等一批珍贵文物。

Twin Pagodas (*Shuangta*), constructed in 982, sits in downtown of Suzhou. The two pagodas are in the same style — seven-layered, octagonal brick pagodas in imitation of a wooden structure. At sunset, the Twin Pagodas look extremely charming.

座落在市区内的双塔,建于公元 982 年。两塔形式相同,均为七层八角仿木楼阁式砖塔。在夕照下,双塔比肩而立,秀美挺拔。

Suzhou has many bridges of various styles. The picture on the left shows the Jade Belt Bridge (*Baodaiqiao*) which is the most graceful ancient stone bridge with many arches still extant in China. Constructed between 817 and 819, it measures 317 meters in length and has 53 arches. The bridge lies on the west bank of the Grand Canal to the south of the city. To build this bridge, the prefecture governor Wang Zhongshu donated his jade belt, hence the bridge got its present name. The picture at the top shows the smallest arched stone bridge in the Fisherman's Garden.

地处水网地带的苏州,城内外造型各异的桥梁举目可见。左为宝带桥,是中国现存古桥中最精美的一座联孔石拱桥,建于公元 817 至 819 年。桥长317 米,有 53 孔,座落在苏州市以南大运河西侧。当时为造桥,苏州刺史王仲舒捐出了自己宝带。上图为城中最小的石拱桥,在网师园内。

Cool Hill Temple, built between 502 and 519, sits beside the Grand Canal in the western part of the city. It is said that Monk Hanshan presided over the temple in the Tang Dynasty, and that is why it is called Cool Hill Temple (*Hanshansi*). Listening to the sound of the bell from this temple is a popular local custom. At midnight, the monks of the temple strike the bell for 108 times, and those who hear the bell sound are said to have calamities driven from them and to have good luck. Many Chinese and foreign tourists make special trips to come to Suzhou so as to listen to the bell on the Eve of the Spring Festival every year.

寒山寺座落在城西古运河旁,建于公元502至519年。相传唐代高僧寒山曾为此寺主持,后人因此称寒山寺。除夕夜半听寒山寺钟声是当地的古俗,当夜寺僧击钟一百零八下,闻者可祛灾纳吉。近年每逢除夕,许多国内外游人专程来寺聆听。

18

The gate of Iron Bell Pass (*Tielingguan*). Outside of the gate is the Fengqiao Bridge over the Grand Canal. The pass was a strategic fortress to protect land and water communications in ancient Suzhou. It was constructed for defending the city from an invasion of Japanese pirates in 1557, during the reign of Jiaqing of the Ming Dynasty.

铁铃关关门。门外就是横跨在古运河上的枫桥。关城扼据于古苏州的水陆要冲,是明嘉靖三十六年(公元 1557 年)为抗御倭寇入侵苏州而建的。

The 16 clay statues of Arhats at the Purple Gold Buddhist Convent (*Zijin'an*) are said to have been made by the famous folk artists, the Lei Chao couples, during the Southern Song Dynasty (1127-1279). The statues have different vivid expressions.

太湖洞庭东山的紫金庵内有16尊泥塑塑罗汉,相传是南宋时(公元1127—1279年)民间雕塑名手雷潮夫妇所塑。塑像的神情富有性格特征。

Red maples on Sky Level Mountain (*Tianping-shan*). The mountain rises about 18 kilometers to the southwest of the city. It is famous for its grotesque rocks, clear springs and ancient maple trees. The scenic spots on the mountain include the Stripe of Sky (*Yitianxian*), Peak that Flew from Afar (*Feilaifeng*), Stone Cave, Stone House and other wonderful views.

天平山枫红时节。天平山座落在城西南18公里处,山势高峻,以怪石、清泉、古枫闻名,并称三绝。山中有一线天、飞来峰、石洞、石屋等奇险景观。

The construction of private gardens in Suzhou started during the 6th century B. C. and was in vogue during the Ming Dynasty (1368-1644). By the end of the Qing Dynasty (1644-1911), there were more than 170 gardens in the city and its suburbs. The city still has a dozen gardens. Fisherman's Garden (*Wangshiyuan*) was constructed in the 12th century and renovated in the 18th century. The eastern part of this garden contains the residential area and the western part is the garden. At the center is a pond with pavilions, towers, covered corridors and halls around it. This is the Pavilion of Moon and Wind (*Yuedaofenglaiting*) at the waterside.

苏州私家建园林始于公元前 6 世纪，至明代建园之风炽盛，清末城内外有 170 多处园林，现存名园十余处。网师园始建于 12 世纪，18 世纪曾重建，园的东部为宅院，西部为园区，园区中部一池碧水，亭轩廊屋环水而筑。图为临水的月到风来亭。

Surging Waves Pavilion (*Canglangting*) was built in the 11th century. Its gate faces a pond, and the buildings inside the garden are all constructed around hills. Ascending the Viewing Hill Tower (*Kanshanlou*), gives you a good view of the distant hills to the southwest of the city. This kind of architectural style is described as "viewing water in front of the gate and borrowing the scene of mountains from outside". This picture shows the scene in front of the garden.

沧浪亭始建于 11 世纪初,园门临水,园内建筑环山布置,登看山楼可览城西南诸峰,因此人们用"园前观水,园外借山"来概括其借景之巧妙。图为园门前景色。

At the entrance to the Pleasure Garden (*Yiyuan*) is a Moon Gate and several loophole windows through which charming scenes inside are sometimes screened and sometimes revealed. This garden was constructed during the late Qing Dynasty and was the last garden built in Suzhou, so it has many of the strong points of other gardens.

怡园入口处,一座月洞门,几扇漏窗,欲障又露,引人入胜。怡园建于清代末期,是苏州现存诸园中建造最晚的一座,故得以吸取众园之长。

Mountain Tower of Containing Jade (*Hanbi-shanfang*) in Lingering Garden (*Liuyuan*) faces a clear pond at its front, where it is the best place to enjoy the lotus flowers in the pond and the moon in the sky. Lingering Garden was the private garden of Xu Taishi, a high official of Taiposhi Banner during the reign of Ming Emperor Jiajing (1522-1566). It later changed hands twice.

留园涵碧山房前临清池，是观荷赏月的最佳处。留园初为明代嘉靖年间(公元1522－1566年)太仆寺卿徐泰时的私家花园,后曾两易其主。

Crown Cloud Peak (*Guanyunfeng*) in Lingering Garden, 6.5 meters high and weighing about 5 tons, is the best of the lake rocks in the gardens of southeast China. The rocks from Taihu Lake have holes in them due to erosion by the water over many years, so they are called lake rocks. They are often seen in imperial gardens where they are used for decoration and scene creation.

留园冠云峰,高6.5米,重5吨,是江南园林湖石之最。太湖中的岩石经浪激波涤,年久形成剔透的空穴,人称湖石。古代皇家园苑多用来点景。

Mandarin Duck Hall (*Yuanyangting*) in Lingering Garden. Lingering Garden is famous for its halls which are usually luxuriously furnished and decorated. This hall is a good example.

留园鸳鸯厅。留园以厅堂宏敞,陈设华丽著称,由此厅可见一斑。

Art Garden (*Yipu*), built in the mid-Ming Dynasty, is small but exquisite. With a big pond, the garden resembles a countryside scene. Here is shown a scene of one courtyard in the garden.

建于明代中叶的艺圃小巧精致,园内水面开阔,颇具江南水乡野趣。图为园内庭院小景。

Lion Grove (*Shizilin*) was built in 1342 during the reign of Emperor Zhizheng of the Yuan Dynasty. It is famous for its artificial hills and caves of different styles.

狮子林建于元代至正二年(公元1342年)。它以假山洞壑取胜,假山造型千姿百态。

Humble Administrator's Garden (*Zhuozhengyuan*) is known as the "Best of the Famous Gardens in Southeast China". Built during the reign of Ming Emperor Zhengde (1506-1521), the garden resembles the natural scenes of southeast China. Water occupies the greater part of the garden. The garden is divided into three sections; east, middle and west. The middle section has the best view. Here is shown the Distant Fragrance Hall (*Yuanxiangtang*) in the middle section.

拙政园享有"江南名园精华"的盛誉。建于明代正德年间(公元1506－1521年)。园中以水为主,具有江南水乡的天然景色。园分东、中、西三部分,以中园景色最佳。图为中园远香堂。

The only covered corridor bridge in the Suzhou gardens is called the Small Flying Rainbow (*Xiaofeihong*). It stands in the middle section of the Humble Administrator's Garden.

这是苏州诸园中独有的一座廊桥,名小飞虹,位于拙政园中园。

◁ Pavilion of Four-side Lotus Wind (*Hefengsimianting*), a hexagonal pavilion, sits in the center of the pond in the middle section of the Humble Administrator's Garden. In summer, lotus grows fully in the pond while winds rise from the water. This is the best place to enjoy the cool breeze.

荷风四面亭,位于拙政园中园水池中央,是一座六角亭。夏日,荷满池塘,清风送爽,为纳凉赏景之处。

Retiring to Thought Garden (*Tuisiyuan*), built in 1885 during the reign of Qing Emperor Guangxu, lies in Tongli Township 27 kilometers to the southeast of Suzhou. With a pond at the center of the garden, the halls, pavilions, corridors and towers are erected beside the pond and look as if they are floating on the water.

退思园位于苏州东南27公里处的同里镇,建于清光绪十一年(公元1885年)。园中以水池为中心,紧贴水面而建的屋宇廊亭,如浮于水上。

①An exquisite brick-carving arch over a gateway.
②A deep lane leading to quiet seclusion.
③Borrowing scenes from outside of the window.
④ The covered corridor rises up and down beside the water, and the window views change as visitors pass by.

①精美的砖雕门楼
②深巷通幽
③窗外借景
④随波起伏的水廊和步移景换的窗景

①	③
②	④

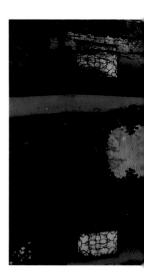

Suzhou gardens have put together all the essences of the private gardens of southeast China. By the Ming and Qing dynasties (1368-1911), the art of garden architecture in Suzhou had reached its summit. This group of pictures show various garden designs and architecture.

苏州园林集中了江南私家园林的精华。到了明清时代苏州的造园艺术达到了巧夺天工的境界。本组图片展示了部分造园手法和建筑技艺。

Viewing the scene in the garden through the exquisitely carved mahogany doorway in the Ladder Cloud Hall (*Tiyunguan*) of Fisherman's Garden.

透过网师园梯云室雕刻精美的红木落地罩,望庭院中景色,犹如一巨幅通景屏。

◁ After 2,000 years, Suzhou is still well-known as a water town. There are waterways totaling 35 kilometers in length, seven north-south rivers and eight east-west ones to form an inner city water network that connects with rivers and lakes outside the city.

历经两千多年，苏州水城风貌依旧。至今城内河道仍达35公里，七条南北向水巷和八条东西向水巷交贯连通，构成了内城水系网络，并与城外河湖相通。

Houses built over a river with covered corridors connecting one to another are a unique architectural style of residential buildings in Suzhou.

跨河建宅，前房后屋以小桥相连，成为水城苏州特有的民居格局。

Boats sailing in the morning glow.
舟行霞光中。

The Beijing-Hangzhou Grand Canal, which was ▷
dug at the beginning of the 7th century, flows
through the southwestern and southern parts of
Suzhou. The river in this area is wide and has
plenty of water, enough to be suitable for navi-
gation.

7世纪初开凿的京杭大运河绕经苏州城的西面和
南面,这段河道宽阔,水量充沛,便于行船。

Year after year，people living on river banks or on boats watch sails passing by and listen to the splashing of water from the oars.

傍河而居的人家或以船为家的船民，日复一日，目送千帆过，耳听橹桨激水声。

In the early morning，old men like to sit in ▷ river-side teahouses drinking tea，listening to birds' singing and viewing the river scene.

清晨，老人们喜欢坐在河畔的茶馆里饮香茶、听鸟鸣、观河景。

Small fishing boats with cormorant can be seen everywhere on the rivers lakes and ponds.

在河塘水荡中常见到用鱼鹰捕鱼的小舟。

A forest of masts at the juncture of river and a lake.

河湖接流处，桅樯林立。

The picturesque Taihu Lake shrouded in mist.
烟波浩淼、风光旖丽的太湖。

Families on boats. The fishermen of Taihu Lake live on boats. Even the domestic fowls raised on these boats can walk skillfully on gangplanks.

水上人家。太湖渔民大都以船为家，生产、生活主要是在船上。连饲养的家禽都能训练有素地沿着狭窄的跳板上下。

One of the famous products of Taihu Lake is whitebait, a kind of thin, long, transparent and tiny fish that is quite delicious. Catching whitebait is one of the major tasks the year around for fishermen of the lake. Here we see them busy in preparing for fishing before the fishing season begins.

太湖盛产银鱼。银鱼体细长、透明,味鲜美,是苏州的名特产。捕捞银鱼是沿湖渔民每年的主要劳作。图为鱼汛前,渔民们在紧张地作准备。

The multiple-sail fishing boats on Taihu Lake are said to have developed from warships in the Ming Dynasty.

太湖中这种多帆渔船相传是由明代海中的战船演变而来的。

◁ The two fishing boats are trawling a net together on the lake. It looks as if they will have a good catch.

两条船张满风帆在合力地拖网作业,看来收获不小。

The East and West Dongting Hills are two pearls in Taihu Lake near Suzhou. Here the scenery is picturesque and the products are abundant. The picture shows spring on West Dongting Hill.

太湖中的东、西洞庭山是太湖近苏州一侧的两颗明珠,这里风景秀丽,物产丰富。图为西洞庭山春天的景色。

There are many kinds of Ming and Qing architecture still found in Dongcun Village on West Dongting Hill. Here is one of the old-style residential houses there. ▷

西洞庭山东村留存有多处明清时代建筑。图为其中一处古色古香的民宅。

There are many ancient townships with different features around Suzhou. The old town of Zhouzhuang to the southeast of the city is one of them. It is surrounded by water and crisscrossed with rivers. The houses are all built on the river banks, and the rivers are spanned by ten stone bridges from the Yuan, Ming and Qing dynasties. The town provides a typical scene of "small bridges, flowing water and households" in southeast China.

苏州城四郊各具特色的古镇数以百计,位于城东南的周庄古镇是其中之一。它四周湖荡环抱,镇内河道纵横,房屋全都沿河而筑,河道上保存着元、明、清历代石桥十座。是典型的江南"小桥、流水、人家"景色。

The old town of Zhouzhuang not only has beautiful scenes but is also a place where many well-known men of letters lived. The town still has about one hundred old houses, among which the "Shenting," "Zhangting" and "Zhouting" are the most famous. The picture on the right is the slabstone-street in front of the "Shenting" House built by a descendent of the rich merchant Shen Wansan during the Ming Dynasty (1368-1644). The picture on the left is a boat on the river in the town.

古镇周庄不仅景色如画,历史上也是人文集萃之地。至今镇上保留近百座古老宅院,其中"沈厅"、"章厅"、"周厅"等最为著名。右图为明代巨富沈万三后裔所建住宅"沈厅"前的青石板街。左图为水镇荡舟。

A rural kindergarten (*left*) and a village girl in a Suzhou-style dress (*below*).

乡村托儿所(左)身着吴装的村姑(下)

Suzhou has a long history of producing arts and handicrafts. They are exquisitely made with many varieties and are known the world over. On the right are sandalwood fans and bone fans painted with traditional Chinese paintings, burnt flowers or pierced patterns. Below artisans can be seen working on a huge embroidery.

苏州工艺美术品历史悠久,做工精巧,品种繁多,享誉海内外,右图为采用"绘画"、"烫花"、"镂空"工艺制作的苏州檀香扇和骨扇精品。下图是工艺师们正在协力制作巨幅刺绣作品。

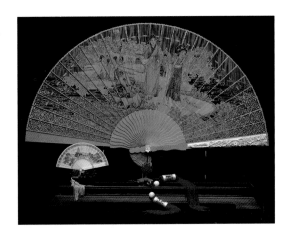

The reconstructed Ganjiang Road connects with the Industrial Garden invested by Singapore in the east and with Suzhou New District in the west. The picture below shows a waterway after being rebuilt.

重新拓宽改建的"干将路",东连新加坡投资兴建的工业园区,西接苏州新城区。下图为整修后的水巷景象。

Sections of the scroll painting *Prosperous Suzhou*. The painting, 1,241 cm long and 39 cm wide, was done in 1759 by Xu Yang, a court painter in the Qing Dynasty, after Emperor Qianlong returned from his second southern inspection tour. This painting vividly depicts the prosperity of the city and the lifestyle of the people 200 years ago.

《姑苏繁华图卷》局部。全图长1241厘米,宽39厘米,清代宫廷画家徐扬作于乾隆二十四年(公元1759年),时值乾隆皇帝第二次南巡不久。画中如实地描绘了二百多年前苏州的繁荣市貌和风土民情。

After returning to Beijing from his southern inspection tours, ▷ Emperor Qianlong ordered the construction of a Suzhou Street at the Summer Palace, which imitates the river town of Suzhou.

乾隆皇帝南巡回到北京后,在颐和园内仿苏州水乡街景建造的苏州街。

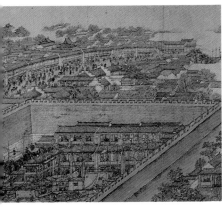

70

A fishing port at sunset.
渔港夕照。

图书在版编目（CIP）数据

苏州：英汉对照/兰佩瑾编辑；吴文撰文。—北京：外文出版社，1998.1
ISBN 7-119-02138-9

Ⅰ．苏…Ⅱ．①兰…②吴…Ⅲ．摄影集-苏州　Ⅳ．J426
中国版本图书馆 CIP 数据核字(97)第 24736 号

Edited by：Lan Peijin
Text by：Wu Wen
Photos by：Niu Songlin　Zhou Rende
　　　　　　Sun Jianpin　Gong Weijian
　　　　　　Lan Peijin　Yao Tianxin
Translated by：Xu Mingjiang
Designed by：Yuan Qing

编辑：兰佩瑾
撰文：吴　文
摄影：牛嵩林　　周仁德
　　　孙建平　　龚威建
　　　兰佩瑾　　姚天新
翻译：徐明强
设计：元　青

First Edition 1998
Second Edition 1999

Third Edition 2000

Suzhou

ISBN 7-119-02138-9

Ⓒ Foreign Languages Press
Published by Foreign Languages Press
24 Baiwanzhuang Road，Beijing 100037，China
Home Page：http://www.flp.com.cn
E-mail Addresses：info @ flp.com.cn
　　　　　　　　sales @ flp.com.cn
Printed in the People's Republic of China

苏　州

兰佩瑾 编

Ⓒ　外文出版社
外文出版社出版
（中国北京百万庄大街 24 号）
邮政编码 100037
外文出版社网页：http://www.flp.com.cn
外文出版社电子邮件地址：info @ flp.com.cn
　　　　　　　　　　　sales @ flp.com.cn
天时印刷(深圳)有限公司印刷
1998 年(24 开)第一版
2000年第一版第三次印刷
（英汉）
ISBN 7-119-02138-9/J・1412(外)
004800（精）